Aim High
My Air Force Experience

by

MSgt Tuebe'd Tzidid
Master Sergeant USAF
Retired

Fulton Books
Meadville, PA

Published by Fulton Books 2024

ISBN 979-8-88982-488-6 (paperback)
ISBN 979-8-89221-015-7 (hardcover)
ISBN 979-8-88982-489-3 (digital)

Printed in the United States of America

Dedication

For putting up with me, forgiving me tolerating me, cooking, cleaning and still loving me after fifty-five years, I dedicate this book to my wife, Iva Goiter. As a career, Iva was a nurse who spent forty-nine years in the smelly trenches of nursing homes, in many cases holding the hands of the dying. Had she been in the military, she'd (with attention to detail, diligence, and compassion) be an excellent first sergeant.

We've faced many problems in five decades. We're still here probably going out to eat too much, probably going to the casino, too much. People say we complement each other.

I can get manic and bothersome, and Iva is laid-back and cool. Whenever I go out to get coffee, go to the bank she always asks if I have my teeth in. She's my proverbial rock who spends her time at her sewing machine making all kinds of things to sell and give to the senior center to sell.

She's Queen Mum of the greatly hated and feared Red Hatters and the first one to tell me to set the table, and it's always a feast. From alligator soup with matzos balls to zebra balls with hyena ears, it's always a celebration in culinary art. I love you, Iva Goiter.

A close second is my shrinkette, Amy. It's been going on for twentysomething years. A wonderful listener with a third-degree blackbelt in feedback and easy to laugh. She's seen me in a mixed bag of symptoms and may've been responsible for having me admitted a couple of times. She'll retire soon, and I'll miss our chats.

To Gabby, thanks for the memories.

To Charles "Chucky" Griswald who was my mentor in Europe and taught me to drive the bug through the Taunus Mountains of Germany.

To Trev, Kami, Peggy Isaacson, Steve Minichiello, Sonny Dufault, Jerry Marder, Lorraine Calzone, John Franchi, Dave Lowell, and Major Ralph Long who (in 1966 for therapy) encouraged me to write about anything I wanted.

I dedicate this book to the 3.999ers who every morning from 1300 to 1400z brighten my days with chatter about anything in fellowship on ham radio.

Finally, I dedicate this book to the memory of Major Edward Delfonzo (RIP) for providing the path to my military retirement.

Seventy-five years old, married for fifty-five years, retired Air Force, Morse code ham radio operator. I love jazz, photography, ham radio, theater, and tripe. In fact, I'm spearheading an organization that'll make tripe a basic food group that can only be satiated at Angelo's in Federal Hill, Providence, Rhode Island. I worked for many years in broadcasting, hosting jazz programs.

In 1965, a senior at Hillhouse High and hardly Harvard-headed, I majored in fantasies—fantasies of being nicely baked while spinning some jazz from the radio room of a tramp steamer off the coast of Bora Bora.

And as a bipolar narcoleptic, I was the captain of the award-winning sleeping/laughing/crying team. Just let it be known I was a wise-ass without a clue, and with the war escalating, the possibility of getting drafted was in such denial that it really never sank in that I could be used in the killing process like I had nothing of which to be concerned. Loving airports and being patriotic, the Air Force seemed to be the place to be. Canada, albeit a beautiful country wasn't a consideration.

When I told folks I wanted to go into the Air Force, they were cautiously concerned, especially with the situation we were in over in Southeast Asia. As million of fathers, my old man told me not to sign anything.

Meanwhile, buddy Marvin, who signed up a year earlier, told me the steps. It was cool to sign those documents in the qualifications process: Interview, test, physical, and then only with my folk's signature, a four-year commitment of travel, growing up, an adventure, health benefits, HOPS, college credits, never giving retirement a thought. Where both folks worked, it was up to me to get the facts and discuss them at dinner.

THE SARGE

Decked out in his class A blues and colorful rack of ribbons the sarge (upon telling him I was a musician) excitedly told me, "…you'll see the world from concert stages!" We broke each other up many times during that first meeting with highly charged, zany, off-the-wall banter.

And as Marvin said, he gave me the skinny on the procedure: first, taking the greatly hated and feared Armed Services Vocational Aptitude Battery (ASVAB) to see if I even academically qualify for the Air Force, whose standards are always higher. After which, audition, physical, and with parents' signature, ship out.

Dinny Banquer, the Hillhouse High School music director and my private clarinet teacher for years was informed by my recruiter that regulations require me to play first clarinet. I didn't. I played bass clarinet, the only one in the band.

Marvin, by the way, was somewhat instrumental in my meeting Gabriella, Gabby for short. In 1963, Marv was an usher at the College Theater. One Saturday matinee, he sneaked buddy Gary and me in through the backstage doors, and while getting popcorn, Gary picked up a couple of dolls to sit with us. Gabby sat with me, and twenty-six years later, we were getting lost in each other's faces.

THE AUDITION

After a lot of practicing scales, arpeggios, études, changes, long tones, and a couple of flute lessons, the audition took place at Westover Air Force Base, Massachusetts, on the second floor of an old, weathered, rickety wooded wartime barracks. The commander, Mr. Berkey, was one of the few Warrant Officers left in the Air Force. Nice guy, looked like Red Skelton, tall, with red hair, kinda goofyish. After our brief conversation, he called his first clarinet to audition me with the usual repertoire: Souza, Mozart, Weber, and a piece the band was working on, Bernstein's Overture to Candide.

Warming up in a soundproof practice room for my shot to wear Air Force Blue, I played a decent glissando to Gershwin's Rhapsody In Blue.

Sounding clarinet credible, the short barrel-chested, chain-smoking leader of the Star Lighters, Master Sergeant Holt, asked me to take out my tenor and laid a special Hal McIntyre Jr. chart of an Ellington tune for me to sight read, and with the comping changes, blow a chorus. Back then, I had read, transpose, and blown chorus chops.

That day, I was given an official AF form stating that I, upon completion of Air Force Basic Training, would be assigned to the 567th AF Band as a woodwind instrumental specialist. It's a good thing. I fared poorly on the ASVAB, barely qualifying for administration with my terrible organizational skills and vehicle maintenance. If it can't be fixed with a hammer, I don't bother with it. I did qualify to be a cook. I'd probably enjoy that.

Fantasies of being the following surfaced:

(1) A host on Armed Forces Network radio or TV service
(2) AF public relations gig at the Pentagon
(3) A photographer
(4) A morse code operator at the top secret facility outside London

PHYSICAL

Three days prior to raising my hand, the results of my enlistment physical determined I was seven-pound underweight. Dr. Larry Chin, the CMO at military enlistment processing station (MEPS) is a rite of passage for anyone who's been or tried to go into the military, told me to tell my mother to get some bananas and beer and come back in three days for weigh-in and ship-out. Why he suggested my mother do this, I've yet to figure out, unless he thought of me as a momma's boy.

Everyone in my circle of friends, family, and teachers was jubilant over this positive life-changing opportunity, except my mother's mother, Nana. She despised Johnson and held him accountable for the mess we were in. At a Yale rally, the old woman angrily tried to rip the badge off a cop. She got arrested while my folks signed their name, allowing me to enlist at the age of seventeen.

THE DAY

July 21, 1965, President Lyndon Johnson met with top aides to confer and come to some answers about the war. It was also the day that I, with my first blinding, throbbing Hulls Beer headache, took the sacred oath to serve, defend the Constitution of the United States from all enemies, foreign and domestic, and bear true faith and allegiance to the same, so help me, yada, yada, yada.

AIR FORCE BASIC TRAINING

Cut to Lackland AFB, San Antonio, Texas, in the oppressively sweltering summer, salt pill-taking heat of Air Force Basic Training. As soon as I landed, I knew in my gut that Texas wasn't going to be a place I'll like.

A deep breath of dry Texas air is a lot different from New Haven, Yale, and Pepe's Pizza air. This Texas air was resplendent with the scent of gunpowder, decaying cattle carcasses, nose-tingling tumbleweed, horse shit, stale beer; and the hell starts as soon as you (in the middle of the night) arrive at reception. Four to five poster sharp training instructors in their command voices screaming, calling us maggots, faggots, and girls.

Six hot and miserable weeks with a bout of cellulitis, my share of eighteen-hour KP, and oh-dark-thirty GI parties where wax stripping the floor is the order of the next two and a half hours. There was a lot of running, jumping, hopping, marching, mud crawling, skipping, and climbing; and one morning, because I didn't shave, a committee (a gathering of vultures) of training instructors (TIs) screaming in my face—an embryonic beard, a two-o'clock shadow.

After this public and horrific experience that brought me to tears, one of the training instructors, a real Southern boy, called me into his office and asked if I wanted out. When I told him I wanted to stay in, "I'm going into the band," he became human, and we chatted about music. I'd expect a no-no, breaking character and all.

When I finally graduated basic, I had to wait for orders, during which time I (the only Jew in the flight) was assigned to manage the squadron's training instructors (TIs) canteen, where I'd order and handle the finances of the candy bars, Twinkies, coffee, etc. After a week or so of that, I—with orders, a stuffed duffel bag, high hopes, wiser, healthier, smarter, focused, savvy, proud, and promoted—came home for a two-week leave donning the stripe of an Airman Third Class and above the left pocket, a National Defense Service ribbon.

My itinerary had me awaiting a connection at Kennedy, where I walked among the uniformed, and there were a lot of us, all branches and ranks.

The USO was hopping with guys crashing overnight. Fresh coffee in a lounge setting, I was greeted courteously and respectfully tended to. Nowhere in that huge terminal did anybody call me a baby killer. It was too early in the game.

HOME

Finally at home, uniformed, spit, and polished, I was the cock of the walk! The Hillhouse High School band went nuts when I showed up at the football game decked out in my tan, short-sleeve, razor-sharp warm weather ware 1505s. But two weeks at home crawled by. With an offer to buy lunch, my recruiter asked me if I'd come into his office a couple of times and talk to kids about basic training. I had nothing else to do. All my buds were in their senior year, with no one to hang with and, even worse, no driver's license.

THE EXIT

The Exit was a small, dimly lit, intimate venue run by the School of Theology at Yale and the place where buddy Larry and I would play in a smoky espresso-smelling venue of a Friday night jazz jam.

We'd play like Trane and Shepp and their sheets of sound. We got close with shits of sound and developed a following. And on this Friday night (with a coke-head pianist), Larry and I got together for the first time in almost two months and rocked the place. A girl I graduated with who never so much as said hello to me said those words: "I had no idea!"

Sitting at a table, enjoying a straight Lucky, a guy comes up to me and says, "My date thinks she knows you," and asks my name. When he told her, she came up to me and gave me a big embrace. It was Gabby, who I haven't seen in months. She looked like someone from heaven with blue eyes, golden hair, and a Camay face with a firecracker scar above her upper lip.

Before my two-week leave was up, the sarge was making a run to the base and offered me a ride. It was time. Excuse me, Edward Albee. The sarge was a "richly comic person," even twenty minutes into the trip when he asked if I had my ID card. Upon checking, I didn't. He had to go back twenty miles to my folk's place. There was no reprimand, no rank-pulling, and no rage. He certainly had reason to be angry. Had I shown up without my ID card, I would've been refused pay and processing, and where Westover was a SAC Base, I could've been denied entrance and/or shot for making the attempt.

WESTOVER AIR FORCE BASE

The words over the main gate at General Curtis LaMay's Westover Air Force Base and emblazoned on the B52s were "Peace Is Our Profession!" With many wet-dream ending alerts, huge bombers would scramble, shaking the barracks while taking off to Hale Eddy.

Readiness in SAC also meant a bed so tightly made a quarter would bounce on it. That would certainly bring the North Vietnamese to their knees.

In the fall of '65, to get young blood into its rank and file, the mission of the band was recruiting, hence high school concerts. In this venue, like the avant-garde great Eric Dolphy, I freely demonstrated the bass clarinet to an auditorium full of potential AF Generals, whom I imagine had never heard a bass clarinet, oboe, etc.

Hal McIntyre Jr., one of the greatest sax players I had ever heard, was in the band. His chart, "Basically Basie" with Chupes on screech trumpet brought about a wonderfully joyful noise in the house every time!

Then there was the healing at the Airman's club. I'm told one of the great trumpet players, Bobby Agnew (who later went with Woody Herman), presented himself as a sightless person with a cane, dark glasses, slow gait, and helper—was healed by another character in the band who was raised fundamentalist and thumped his way through King James.

The entire miracle was fueled by nickel beers. Word got around that there really was healing, increasing attendance at the base churches that Sunday. If we didn't have any weekend gigs and if I wasn't CQ (charge of quarters), I'd invite one of the guys home, where they'd get a home-cooked Swanson TV dinner and a trip to the Exit, where they would join the festivities.

Air shows, TV shows, state fairs, radio programs, parades, retreats, park concerts, senior centers, hangings, combo gigs at the officer's club, we did it all, and last but not least… moral for the troops.

In a biting, freezing subzero December, we, in a C47, flew on a humanitarian mission to tropical, sea-breezed, coconut-scented Ramey Air Force Base, Puerto Rico, where a carton of straight Lucky went for $.99 at the BX. We were there to perform at a conference of generals, who just so happened brought their wives, girlfriends, and golf clubs. Yup, it was up to the band to keep up morale.

On a two-day trip to a dark Harmon AFB, Newfoundland, I met and fell hopelessly in love with brown hair in bangs Michelle Kubiak, a USO singer/dancer from Astoria, Long Island, New York. I pined deeply for a couple of weeks with calls to her on the official telephone line of the Department of Defense, the AUTOVON line. Two weeks later, realizing futility, it was over.

Coincidentally, that's when I met Iva, my roommate's fiancé, my wife of fifty-five years. My roommate was a slob from Seattle who stank and never cleaned nor swept his area. Anyway, they were engaged, and they'd invite me to tag along for coffee, ice cream, burgers, etc. When the slob got orders to go to Japan unaccompanied, he insisted she go live with his mother in Seattle. Well, that wasn't her agenda, and they broke up, and we became good friends.

WIESBADEN, GERMANY

After a year of high school concerts, my wanderlust was getting the best of me, so I put in for an overseas assignment, and three weeks later, I was given orders to a three-year tour with the United States Air Force Europe (USAFE) Band in Wiesbaden, Germany.

The night before leaving, my folks had a going-away party for me where I told everyone of my plans to marry the gorgeous, ever-present, in-my-mind Gabby, at which point my father and favorite uncle (living their life vicariously through me) got into my "getting married" case, insisting I have a great time in Europe.

When I was thirteen, my favorite uncle gave me the greatest material gift ever: a portable, six-transistor AM radio that under covers took me all over North America as I ever so slowly tuned the dial. This developed my desire to someday work in broadcasting. I'd methodically write to the chief engineer of these stations, telling them what I heard at exact times along with technical info that would be useful to them. In return, they'd send me QSL cards—impressively logoed postcards as confirmation of my report. Thirty-seven states and five Canadian provinces were confirmed on that little radio.

Anyway, the next day, my father drove me to McGuire AFB, New Jersey, for a night flight to Frankfort, where the first thing you see as you're making the early-morning approach to Rein-Maine are stacks. Black-smoking, air-polluting, loogy-producing stacks; and on a miserable day, it's heavy with it. Yet, looking wide-eyed, sickened, and perplexed (you try it), a lieutenant colonel asked me if I wanted a ride to the base. I couldn't pass that up.

The ride to Lindsey Air Station downtown Wiesbaden was on the autobahn, where there was no speed limit and no wrecks to behold. After dropping off my records, where they will be updated and filed, I got paid and hopped the shuttle to the air base, where finally I met the commander, a brilliant jazz pianist who also knew his way around a baton. A man who changed my life forever, Major Ed Delfonso, God rest his soul.

On my first night in Germany, I dressed in my three-piece suit and was psyched for an exciting adventure. The shuttle from the air base to downtown Wiesbaden ran on a frequent schedule, and for the first time since my visits to New York City, I felt like a tourist—wide-eyed, mouth agape, and eager for my 1st German meal.

'Twas an eatery on a cobblestone street not far from the *Bahnhof* (railroad station), a very quaint venue that enticed me with the scent of warm pumpernickel bread fresh out of the oven. An attractive young waitress, a brunette in her early twenties, modestly dressed, led me to a table by a window overlooking the old milk path. As I was checking everything out, the waitress showed a young well-dressed couple to a table near me. As I was trying to make sense of the menu, the young man (Wolff) asked me something in German, and all I could say was "*Nich fershtein.*" ("I don't understand.")

That opened an evening of wonderful laughter from one and all as we butchered our paper currencies with editorial yah-and-nay gestures depending on the likeness on the bill, and I had my first of many *jager schnitzels,* and to this day Baba Bier with hops kissed by the angels (*mit Steinhäger)* set the *bier* and schnapps standard for me.

The young couple, Wolff and Anna, were on their way to the *Kurhaus,* a lavish (out of Jame Bond) casino, and asked if I wanted to join them. I begged off and never saw them again.

The barracks, rehearsal hall, and recording studio were in the same building around the corner from the Nimbus Club. 'Twas there where a slot machine quickly ate up $7 and my spirits (lest we forget nickel beers on Wednesday). The acts, however, were first-class musicians who did military bases and cruises. One group transcribed Buddy Rich's "West Side Story" to three horns and rhythm and cooked for over eight minutes.

On one of the three air corridors that were agreed upon after World War II, it was nothing for us to fly into *Tempelhof*, Berlin, for three days of a parade and concerts. On my first time there, we took a bus tour with an armed East German guard. Looking into the eastern sector from the Brandenburg Gate, armed East German guards on watch towers were keeping a vigilant eye on things. The city was still war-torn.

There were really no traffic and few people. We were advised not to take the rapid transit as it goes into the eastern sector and, if caught, would probably stand trial for spying. And where I recently found the lost chord and sworn to its secrecy, they would've tortured me. I hate that!

On the Fourth of July, we'd perform at the Danish-American festival in Aalborg/Skagen, Denmark, and share the stage with the likes of Borge. It was here where I burned lobster red from lying on a beach where the North and Baltic Seas meet.

A dude in the band, whom I couldn't stand and whom I was quite rude to because his face was always a blur (don't ask) sympathetically came to my rescue like someone from heaven. He had no reason to tend to me, but he did, and needless to say, my attitude about him and all blurred-faced people changed.

Well, next to a kidney stone, that sunburn had to be a close second, burning up and itchy, making scratching a torturous Chinese hell.

Barely able to make rehearsals, if I went to the dispensary, they'd be obligated to prefer charges for destroying government property. It was tacitly understood that I was going to go through this without medical attention. Now on a four-day trip to Oslo, I lost eight pounds from not eating. The herring should be on their nation's flag.

Gabby and I were writing frequently before her dear John, where she told me she was engaged to a doctor. Oh well, I was in Europe!

My recruiter, now in fatigues was stationed across the street from the band barracks. He was right. I was seeing the world from concert stages. When we banged into each other at the German canteen (where the *schnitzel mit pomfrets* and salad was *schmect*), he invited me to his place for Sunday dinner after going to church with him and his family.

At the time, it sounded like a plan. With all his imagined pre-approach to the wife, I anticipated they were both expecting me to be funny. The zany banter wasn't there. It just wasn't in me. It was another time. Uncomfortable, all I wanted to do was get the hell out of there. Fortunately, he lived on the shuttle bus route back to the base. Feeling very low, confused, guilty, and ashamed, I, with some excuse about a gig at the officer's club, left and never saw him again.

WOODY HERMAN

While growing up in New Haven, Sonny Costanzo was a music mentor to a lot of us kids. Weekly, more than twenty of us would run down the hip book of Gene Hull charts. Sonny, in 1967, was with Woody's Thundering Herd and scheduled to play at Rhein-Main-Halle in Frankfurt. One of my bandmates would supply the transportation if I bought him a ticket. And wanting the company of a woman who speaks English, I called an information operator and asked her if she'd be my date. We met there.

The band cooked, wailed, smoked, and screamed for over two hours. At intermission, Helga and I went backstage to see Sonny. Overjoyed and surprised, he introduced us to the players, where every word uttered by frantic tenorman was "fuckin' reed, fuckin' mouthpiece." It was kinda scary. We left in a start. At the end of the concert, I went up to Sonny to express the awe of the evening, and there was Helga, walking off with Woody. Years later, I was an MC at a series of jazz concerts, and Woody was featured. I called him on it, and with his eyeballs going to the upper right, he was taking a long, slow smile.

CHUCKY GRISWALD

In the spring of '67, Charles "Chucky" Griswald signed on as pianist, arranger, and the best cymbal player I ever marched to. To this day, he's my oldest, dearest friend. After a morning rehearsal, Chucky invites me to his apartment in town to have dinner with his wife and one-year-old daughter.

"Bring your bass clarinet," he said.

I did and also experienced for the first time the pleasure, ecstasy, the heavenly enveloping warmth of dark Moroccan-opiated hashish.

My personal life was in shambles: parents divorcing, being homesick, and no real religious values to keep me charged while keeping up with the rigors of the schedule. I started to lose it in depression.

Doctor (major) Ralph Long, PhD a hi-fi buff and AF psychologist I was seeing for that and the pangs of growing up, became a surrogate father, showing up at local concerts with his wife and kids. His treatment would require me to write every day about whatever I wanted, including my Pulitzer Prize paragraph on my Berlin devirgination. We spoke about it. It was time, and I was going to Berlin where, after some inquiry from other band members, the price in 1967 was 50 deutsche marks, $12.50. And I wouldn't settle for any less than Gabby's twin. And it was. I didn't have to walk very far.

MY DEVIRGINATION

Taking the last drag from a Roth Handle cigarette, there she was—a fifty-bit whore, five foot three, a micro miniskirted millimeter from pubic hairs, maybe eighteen years old, blonde with blue eyes, slight of build, and come-hither I would experience with Gabby decades later. The venue was on the third floor of a cold water flat with torn-shaded windows, a single bed, peeling wallpaper, a night-stand on which were rubbers, and on the door, a hook for my pants.

My first *schmushki*, and with a real blonde, I was up for it (as it were) posed, poised, and proud. With her top still on and me with extra-large rubbah, I went in! Doing what comes naturally, nothing, I was feeling nothing—no kisses, no warm embrace, no simultaneous breathing, nothing that'll make for a wonderful memory or an orgasm. After a while, this aerobic activity that could've taken place in a meat locker came to a halt. Riding myself of the extra-extra-large rubbah, she jerked me off, and that was that. Gloating and perplexed, I returned to my *Tempelhof* room, where I felt grown-up, worthy, and able to share in the ribald.

THE TRAVEL AGENT

In 1967, a travel agent was a place where people buy and trip, and in this case was on the eighth floor of the brick building over Uncle Horst's *Wursthaus*, where twice a month on payday, we'd drive the bug to Frankfurt. The last time we were there, a college kid tripped out on acid, yelling, screaming, swearing, laughing, and pushing those in his path out of the way before he nose-dived out the open window.

Screaming, everyone scattered for exits. After what seemed like forever, the elevator finally arrived and, on the descent, stopped between the sixth and fifth floors. Quite stoned, Chucky, I, and an international cast of characters hacked, coughed, cried and prayed. Finally, the elevator lowered to the first floor, where upon opening, three gorilla-like, axe-wielding German Politzi shoved us out of the way for their ride up.

THE HOLY GRAIL OF SHIT

On a five-day trip to an international trade fair in Kabul, Afghanistan, three trombone players, for an undisclosed amount and at great risk, stashed a pound of hash a piece in their trombone cases, the street value of which back then would be a healthy five figures. Every day for months, we'd show up stoned. The only time anyone said anything was at a social function where dress civvies were required. We were under the influence and accustomed to being with people and savvy enough to act normally.

The Ben Webster sound-alike first sergeant came up to us and casually asked, "How'd you get so nice?"

I treated it as something rhetorical and blew it off. He actually didn't want to know. With the exception of the five to six guys we turned on, nobody was the wiser. During all this, Chucky's wife and daughter went back to the States, and we became barracks roommates.

CHUCKY, MY MENTOR

My twenty-four-month buzz was a memorable black hole! Chucky rented a piano for the room and would blow tunes, bop, standards, and blues after the workday. He did everything: painting, graphic design, teaching voice, piano, flute, bagpipes, accordion, and spoons. As for his piano chops, he's been called the Second Coming of Bill Evans. Nothing wrong with that!

During this, my celebrated stoned period, he taught me to drive standard through the *Taunus* mountains. Occasionally we'd go to the Catacombs, a jazz joint in Mainz, and jam with a German rhythm section. Guitar great Phil Upchurch would stop by.

A troop train we took from Frankfurt to West Berlin was an overnight when, at the allied border, machine-gunned East German politzi with East German shepherds checked the car's underbelly, making sure that no one was escaping to the western sector.

On another occasion, we were flying over communist East Germany en route to West Berlin. This day, I dropped a lighted smelly *Gauloises* French cigarette between the seats. Disbelief, sudden belief, panic, and in his attempt to find the lit butt through my hysterics, he physically grabbed me by both hands on my arms and shook me, telling me to "snap out-of-it." That had to be the most terrifying moment of my life, imagining we'd crash and burn and, if survived, be sent to Siberia. *Nyet!*

Berlin was always a ball. Good jazz clubs, Carmel Jones, good bier, yager schnitzel, elevators that went sideways, and by those who congregated at various venues off the Kdam, a travel agent was always a block away.

Radio-wise, a black DJ was thrown out of the Army, made his home in East Berlin and, while touting the advantages of his new home, played some decent jazz, all black musicians. Painting a picture of how wonderful his life was over there, he was encouraging black GIs/expatriates to make a move.

On Armed Forces Network (AFN), a host on his program played the best version of "Stardust" I had ever heard. Mesmerizing Tony Scott on clarinet changed me musically. It really opened my ears.

Within the band, there was a cast of characters: winners and losers. One of the losers was dating absolutely the worse person he should have anything to do with, the daughter of the Office of Special Investigations (OSI) commander, and for a blow job said the following to his lady love, "If you're interested in getting some hashish, I know where we'd score."

THE BUST AND JURISPRUDENCE

Enter two plainclothes men, Special Agents Black and White. Agent Black was Caucasian, and Agent White was Afro-American. Like every night, we were with the cosmos, and as luck would have it, we smoked our last gram and were really not aware of the gravity of the situation and being too wrecked to come to our own defense.

Consequently, under their "good cop, bad cop" approach, we spilled our guts and the guts of those who smoked with us, and we signed confessions. Taking our pipe and cleaning accessories, the agents left, allowing us to stay with the band on our own recognizance while the military churns out justice. In the meantime, smoke-wise, there was a guy who was thrown out of the Army, lived in Mainz, and he always had some good shit.

Armed in my defense with a soft cover edition of *The Marijuana Papers*, my lawyer said it wouldn't be prudent for me to testify. After all the jurisprudence, I was found quite guilty of fourteen specifications of use, transfer, and possession by a general (firing squad) courts-martial that dolled out a year and a dishonorable discharge.

Meanwhile, Major Delfonzo said during the trial, "I'd take him back provided he was rehabilitated," and signed a statement attesting to that.

When the cop went to apply the cuffs on me, the JAG, a full bird colonel, said, "That won't be necessary."

On December 7, 1968, I spent my twenty-first birthday in jail.

The local American newspaper *Overseas Weekly* had a photo-filled field day with Chucky and me, and it also gave me the opportunity to take the heat off the band by informing readers that I was sorry for besmirching the reputation of the unit. Major DelFonzo thanked me for that. He knew.

BUSH'S BASTILLE

Bush's Bastille was so named 'cuz he was the NCOIC of a small jailhouse and diesel stop in Mainz. Oscar, a guy in the next cell, was charged and awaiting trial for selling guns to the Czechoslovakian underground.

One morning, around 2:00 a.m., a car crashed through the barricade and fired live rounds into his cell. Nobody got hurt, and the driver got away. The whole thing took fifteen seconds tops.

Having spent a year plus in SAC, loud noises didn't bother me. Chucky told me what happened. In no less than twenty minutes, security police were placed around the Bastille.

On the upside, Sundays were especially warm when folks from the band and their wives would visit us with baked goodies. One of the wives made a cake shaped like a knife. The guard thought that was pretty funny and joined us in its chocolate goodness.

Don't ask me how it got there. A mound of clay that I could squeeze 'tween my fingers was pretty anal. It was accessible, and I respectfully fashioned a crucifix from memory. When Bush saw it, he asked me what that was. With utmost respect, I told him it was my take on a crucifix. Paperwork was filled out, saying I was mentally ill. Ya think?

RAMSTEIN AIR BASE JAIL

After a month in Bush's Bastille, we were sent to a real correctional facility at Ramstein Air Base, where every morning, we stood inspection and did shit work cleaning the base, trimming the grass, menial stuff, and every week, a chaplain would come by and talk to us.

A more scholarly than people-oriented rabbi dropped by and spoke from the Kabbalah, the book of Jewish mysticism, leaving the twelve of us incarcerated scratching our heads, asking each other, "What the fuck was that all about?" An embarrassed Jewish kid said he's gonna sew on a foreskin when he gets out. During this time, I gained strength and inspiration from reading *Atlas Shrugged*. If you're in the slam, love railroads, and individualism, it's a must-read.

Based on our outstanding job evaluations, the government approved clemency, sending Chucky and me to a congressionally scrutinized AF correction/rehabilitation facility at Lowry AFB in Denver. Important people in Washington were very interested in the Air Force's 3320th Retraining Group.

The day finally arrived when we were given orders back to the States to be rehabilitated in the Rocky Mountain High of Denver. By this time, I was on some heavy-duty meds for depression. When I reported to the charge of quarters (CQ), I handed over all my amber plastic bottles with Valium and was told, "The doc will discuss these with you in the morning!"

No more barred living but open bay barracks with bunk beds. One retrainee will make the national news when he takes part in a peace rally while in uniform. High-profile stuff.

The staff? Highly trained NCOs and civilians with psych degrees who were damn nice people. Nothing like an anticipated basic training. One sarge took a group of us to a golden gloves match. Once a month, we'd go to Fitzsimmons VA hospital, where we'd assist the nurses on the chaotic amputee ward…worth a million zillion special indulgences.

After weeks of group therapies, AF training films, speed reading course, and shrink appointments, a civilian third-world psychologist (all the AF could afford that year) suggested I wanted to sleep with my mother. When I told him I wanted to sleep with *his* mother, he, after shock, spewed off something in his native tongue and frantically pointed to the door. The next morning, I was ordered to meet with the head shrink, a colonel who, in my face, told me my remark was uncalled for and ordered me to apologize for my disrespectful flippancy, and the son of a bitch is starting to laugh. Another finger pointed at the door. Toward the end of my total 242 days of confinement, I extended for a year to get out honorably.

My audition to get back into the band career field was terrible, like I never played. So I cross trained to yet another Air Force Specialty Code (AFSC) Recreation Specialist, where they needed my services at a base scheduled to close in a year.

Niagara Falls International Airport

My gig? Work for a girth-blessed civilian woman GS something, and it was awful as she attempted to push her tonnage around. The upside required me to write for the base newspaper, informing one and all about coming events at the service club like bingo, a dance, horseback riding, whatever. If it was a dance, I had to round up girls from Buffalo (not as good as it sounds) and set up their transportation. It was a comfortable and quiet base.

On those days when I had nothing to really do, I'd take leave. Uniformed, I'd pay $72 for a round-trip ticket on Mohawk Airlines from Buffalo to Hartford. Iva would pick me up, and we'd hang out for a couple of days, or she'd fly into Buffalo, and we'd go to Toronto for a weekend.

With the mist of the falls beading on my face and a high school photo of Gabby still in my wallet, I, with a $70 ring from the BX, asked Iva Goiter the universal question and got a "Sure, why not!" On December 31, 1969, we jumped over a broom in front of a Justice of the Peace and moved into our first crib owned by a couple who also owned a deli. On the first of the month, we'd go there to pay the $70 rent and were always given a wonderful take-home package of freshly imported cheese and cold cuts.

One morning after opening up the service club, I was messing around on the piano, and unbeknownst to me, the base commander was listening, and I, like a fool, never got up and stood at attention. Word got around about that.

It was he who extended his hand, and we chatted, and he asked if I'd be interested in playing lounge piano a couple of nights a week in the officer's club. I accepted. Money was good. (Come to find out, this colonel was the commander of the retraining squadron Chucky and I were assigned to for head shrinking and rehabilitating.) By the way, Chucky went back into the Air Force band system and got out honorably—more about him to follow.

Meanwhile, my piano-playing prowess was more of a visual experience as I assumed the affect of being one with the instrument. Hunched over, head cocked to one side, intensely listening. I lost the gig when a colonel's wife wanted to hear Beer Barrel Polka, and once again, I went through all the head gyrations. Finally, when I went to get my pay, I was told that was my last night.

The base was about to close, and my year extension for an honorable had arrived. To cover a square, I was given a retention interview, at which time I told the sarge I'd re-up if I could go to the Broadcast School at Fort Benjamin Harrison, Missouri. 'Twas a dream where I imagined a tour with Armed Forces Network Berlin, Germany. It never came to be, and I was already scheduled under the GI Bill to attend a now-defunct college in Boston, Grahm Junior College as a TV production major. Outrageous comic performance artist Andy Kaufman graduated a year before me in 1971.

For the two months before school, I worked with my father-in-law at a Connecticut River, polluting paper mill in Holyoke, Massachusetts. I was a lackey getting materials for the guys actually making paper—a job that I swore I'd never have to do again and a job that inspired me to study hard at school.

Grahm Junior College was a wonderful school where I did my share of jazz radio on WCSB close circuit to the Kenmore Square real estate and had my first jazz interview, which resulted in a psychotic breakdown of gut-wrenching uncontrollable hysterics, bawling at the desk of Bob Loxly, whose gig was to help troubled students. In the last analysis, it was fear. Jazz-wise, I was talking the talk. Could I walk the walk? That was the question.

Hysteria

Here, I was going to interview a legend, and the prevailing thought of *Do I really want to do this for* a living? *Am I going to be good at it? Why am I doing this?* hung like an albatross. I felt trapped, insecure about my goals, and frightened of the future.

I have no idea how I ended up in his office. Maybe it was a guidance notice on a school corkboard. Bawling hysterically, he set me up with a shrink appointment at a state facility a couple of miles away. To burn off steam, I walked/ran. When I finally made it to the doc, I was shaky but able to tell him convincingly I wasn't going to kill myself. With that said, he let me go home, where I got stoned with college kids down the hall. It was either a high-grade smoke or the fragile state of my mind that caused me to panic with an over-powering anxiety attack, raised out-of-control voice, and hysterical screams of dying. Iva called an ambulance, which took me to the same state facility where, this time, I talked about existentialism. All this resulted in my first of many group therapies. That's another book.

MOSE

The late Mose Allison was the cause. While staying at the Copley Plaza, he was working at Paul's Mall on fashionable Boylston Street. One of my teachers, Jeff Fox, suggested I interview the gentleman. With some abysmal, deeply rooted trepidation, I made the appointment for ten o'clock the next morning. Jeff gave me a crash course in operating a Teac reel-reel duel mic stereo tape recorder. When I made it to the Plaza, I went to the bar for a shot. I remember the bartender asking me, "What'll you have?" "Whiskey, I'll have a whiskey thank you." That's the way they did it on *Gunsmoke*.

Let it be said Mose Allison was one of the nicest people I've interviewed. He was an unassuming, soft-spoken Southern gentleman who, for over sixty years, played piano to international audiences, uniquely having his way with words and music (and was not a Sinatra fan). As Mose wrote, "*Your mind is on vacation, and your mouth is workin' over time.*" Then there was an interview with Bill Evans in the sack with a pretty lady in a sleazy motel in Chelsea.

As a TV production major, I produced a series of one-hour shows called *Jazz from the 'Combs* after the club in Mainz. After one meeting with the crew, I told them what I wanted for a set, and seventy-two hours later, we took to the air of Grahm Junior College.

The students and faculty at Berklee would supply the musicians. Bassist Ron McClure came in with the best tenor player (as determined by Downbeat) in Norway and blew everybody away with his frantic fiery solos. And lest we forget lighting, audio, cameras, floor director, and technical director. Something I'd do forty-one years later.

In 1972, with an associate's degree and Honor Society lapel pin, I got a job at channel 7 in the public affairs end of things. Radio and TV stations had to renew their licenses every five to seven years, and they had to show what they've done to better serve those in their coverage area. Channel 7 was the only station in Boston that offered tours of their facility, and I was their docent. Community relations would go into the inner city to identify problems. Three days a week, and invites to station functions, not too shabby.

Coming to the realization of no upward mobility, I left and moved thirty-five miles southwest, where I got a job at a flea power AM station. It was here where I met Sonny Dufault, one of the most respected radio producers in the business. With my copy, Sonny and I produced radio spots that were humorous and worked well for the station's advertisers. In 1991, we produced award-winning radio interviews with famous songwriters—a very fertile time.

In November 1974, Gerald entered the world in spite of me and my hands-off policy in child raising, grew up to be a mensch, and I'm happy to say, is happily married; and after all the years of obsessive worry, he's doing well, enjoying life, and that's a prayer answered. At this writing, no grandkids. All my friends have 'em.

AIR NATIONAL GUARD

Taking doctors and nurses to their assigned hospitals and nursing homes, the Blizzard of '78 was good press for the National Guard. The official AF form signed by Major Delfonzo stating in the record he'd take me back into the band allowed me to come back into the Air Force family; in this case, the fifth largest Air Force in the world, the Air National Guard, assigned to the Band of Cape Cod. A civilian sixteen-piece dance band I was working with got my chops in a good place, making an audition a walk in the park. When I confessed to having suffered depression, they needed a letter from my shrink saying that I no longer have it.

As a result of my checkered AF history, my DD 214 gave me a reenlistment code that required a waiver by the State AG. A week after making the application and getting a physical, it was approved. My physical was being questioned by the charge nurse, where I admitted that insanity runs on both sides of my family. When I told her I was going into the band, she said, "What the hell. Have fun!"

One weekend a month and two weeks during the year, I'd keep my shoes spit-shined and look like a recruiting poster. It was a farcical experience where everyone except the friendly, filing folks in Admin would simply crash on the carpeted floor while those of us who wanted to play music were told to use the soundproof practice rooms. The commander was a good trumpetman and conductor who got his doctorates via mail from some college in England. His diploma said he did *jolly good*!

We worked the internationally known Falmouth Road Race, nursing homes, and evening Fourth of July park concerts where the bugs were so numerous they obstructed the lighting. One weekend in an Air National Guard C130, we flew to Louisville for a parade and concert in their Civic Center.

One weekend a month for three years showing up in a professional manner, I was asked by Major Visconti if I would be interested in being a full-time recruiter. Financially, I couldn't afford not to. Free health care for the family, retirement, and rank, what could I say?

RECRUITING SCHOOL

Recruiting school was back at Lackland for six weeks of Air Force active duty as a staff sergeant. There were ten of us—the ten who dared! Nine passed. Shortly after recruiting school, I received orders for a four-year tour as a full-time Air National Guard recruiter. Elation over a steady paycheck, hundreds more than what I was getting at the station, and coming back to the Air Force family, I renewed a professional relationship with a dry cleaner.

One morning in the shower, while brushing my teeth, my toothbrush missed my mouth and went into my eye, scraping the hell out of my cornea, causing me to go to the Army Hospital at Fort Devens. When Iva said the following, it made it a less painful day.

"It's a good thing you weren't flossing. You would've hanged yourself!"

What a mind. The doc gave me some shit to put in it and a patch, and I developed an insatiable urge to sell shirts.

John, my first boss, could bring 'em in. He received an award for sending a flight (twenty or so kids) to basic training all at the same time. Pretty good, if you can do it, lot of logistics. He played the system well. Then there was the day he was yelling and screaming at me, and he got a phone call from his boss, informing him he was no longer my supervisor. My new boss was the commander of the squadron I was assigned, a very religious man. Both of them are now deacons in their church, and that's good. Deities needs all the loving souls they can touch. I can see it now, Pope John the Recruiter.

Carol, my office partner for eight years, was a great recruiter and is, to this day, a dear friend. Oftentimes, we'd go TDY (temporary duty) to conferences around the country. In Albuquerque, we hopped a city bus to take us to the downtown district. The driver went off route and showed us the local neighborhoods. He'd loop around bus stops, eventually picking up passengers.

The annual Air National Guard Recruiter Conference was hosted by a different state. The one in the Pittsburgh area featured a recruiter from a frigid-in-winter state where tobogganing is popular. This recruiter raced in an Olympic event, and he tiredly went on and on as a supposedly motivational speaker. It was awful.

A military dining-in is an age-old tradition where formal dress (military tux) is required and booze and cigars for either sex are plentiful. I was the facilitator, the MC. It's a high-spirited morale boost from general to cadre. There were some great times. I worked with some wonderfully beautiful people who I'd love to see again.

Lest I forget the frequent TDY to places all over the country for seminars, advanced management training, and an occasional assist at the Guard Bureau at Andrews Air Force Base, Maryland, where one TDY took me there to assist at a conference of religious broadcasters. I was there to get these folks to play Air National Guard Public Service Announcements (PSAs). I ended up being a sound bite on the Voice of America.

A week before going, I called the US Information Agency (Voice of America) to set up a time to meet one of my heroes, Willis Conover, a jazz institution. It was he who brought jazz to all corners of the world on the Voice and could arguably be responsible for the downfall of communism in the Eastern Bloc, where jazz was outlawed.

In the '50s, when the cold war was asimmerin', Willis's program was being jammed by Russia where jazz was illegal to listen to or play. There came the day someone told someone told someone that jazz was the music of the working class. The jamming became an infrequent occurrence.

Anyway, a day after my call, Iva gets called from them inquiring as to who I am. After coming to the conclusion I was a harmless jazz fan, they directed me to take the tour, after which I'll meet with my hero. Everything went off like clockwork. He met with me and took me to the studio where he was broadcasting to the Warsaw countries where Jazz was illegal to play and listen to. What chops! His patter was delivered at a very slow, perfectly enunciated pace with *basso profundo* pipes. It was called Special English. And he couldn't have been more of a gentleman.

After introducing a Freddie Hubbard cut, and telling his listeners the session was three-thousand miles away from the last Charlie Byrd recording I asked him why he refers to the distance in miles. "Wouldn't it seem more proper to say it in kilometers? They don't know from miles." With a burning butt 'tween his nicotine-stained fingers, he said in his own enviable way, "…because this, is the voice, of America."

One long weekend, thanks to the New Hampshire Air National Guard, John and I hopped on a KC135 navigational training flight/refueling mission to Hawaii. Those who wanted to ski were dropped off in Utah. Laying on a beach overlooking Diamond Head I saw my first thong perfectly presented on a young bride honeymooning. On another occasion, I, in a Rhode Island Air National Guard C130, flew to Travis Air Force Base, California, to visit Chucky in Berkeley.

In 1983, fourteen years had gone by. There were no letter writing and no Christmas cards. From one of my old radio advertising clients, I found out he was playing piano in the bay area. I called him, and we chatted about the old days and the deaths of a buddy of ours and the asshole who got us busted. Suicide!

When I told him there was a flight to Travis, he suggested I take it and hop the bus from there to San Francisco and the BART to Berkeley, where he was living. It sounded like a plan. The plane with web seats along the perimeter was worth every cent ($0). With two stops, it took eighteen hours to get to Travis via Memphis, and it took very little to say that's my last time flying in one of those damn things.

It was my first time on the coast, my first sushi, my first saki while marijuana-free since putting the uniform back on. It was a wonderful hang sightseeing, picture-taking, listening to his playing, eating Afghani food for the first time, and getting away from home for a long weekend. Rather than flying back on the 130, I booked passage on Pan Am.

Over the years while making some inquiries I got Gabby's phone number and gave her a jingle. Had a guy answered, I was quite prepared to tell him, "We went out when we were kids." Anyway, she answered and was thrilled. We scheduled a meeting at her snooty address in Stevensonburgville City.

When we met, she made me a tuna fish sandwich on white, topped with a quart of mayonnaise. She was nervous. A year later, I moved out and onward.

With Gabby in my life, free, madly in love, undiagnosed, sans meds, we gave each other what our marriages lacked and assumed the affect of performing seals wherever we went. It was also my celebrated Robert Schumann (1810–1856) period, resplendent with periods of cycled bawling, hysterics, deep sadness, and exuberance. It was a mixed state psychosis with in-the-wind invincibility and tearful, fearful, despondent, and miserable depression. Nine months of (excuse me, Mr. Dickens) *the best of times, the worst of times*. A feverishly intense connection of passion, longing, needing (can't forget that), celebrating, loving, traveling, and some real serious eye gazing as I envisioned us living in a log cabin in Times Square. Don't ask. Between the two of us, we bought out all of Hallmark's "I Thank God You're Alive" selections.

We were kids when I took her to see The Ten Commandments. It was also the day I gave her a friendship ring. While DeMille was giving Heston the Laws, the friendship ring fell onto the sticky floor, and while searching for it, we missed numbers 7 and 10. Twenty years later, it took on a life of its own. It was a seven ten split.

THE GIG

One of the worse parts of the job was cold-calling, especially while feeling like shit. I never did like talking on the phone. Calling prior service folks was less of a problem where they were already in at one time and knew the poop. Kids required another approach.

Anyway, I took a prior service applicant to MEPS for his physical. It was here where he told the doctor he took over a hundred acid trips, disqualifying him. Months later, I was able to get him checked out elsewhere, where he said nothing of his acid days. As a lineman, he was one of the best troops in the unit.

THE JOB

What I'm about to tell you is that you should go no further than us.

I had an early morning appointment with a prior service AF lineman forty miles away, where he was needed by the squadron. 'twas a frigid, snowy, and dark January at 0530 in the north county, and taking 3 straight-up flights of stairs was exhausting and painful. Upon knocking at his door, he said, "Come in. I'm in the living room." And there he was in his underwear sporting a morning woody.

Now I've posed to friends the question, What would you do? Gay friends responded with, "Oh my, continue!"

My straight veteran buddies all said, "Get the fuck outta there."

Running with a side of paranoia, I thought I was being framed by headquarters. With that in mind, I kept eye contact for twenty minutes, enough time to fill out a signed interview card. Disgusted with the job, I simply came to the conclusion that the son-of-a-bitch had a hard-on for the Air National Guard. When I told the construction chief what happened, he said, "We don't need him."

Securing $70,000 worth of free PSA time on Boston TV, they gave me the Air Force Achievement Medal. The money was as easy as giving the Public Service Director at channel 7 a call for an appointment. When she told me it would be her birthday, I bought her a rose. She told all her contemporaries, and before you knew it, all the stations in Boston were playing our PSAs and in premium times like during *Law and Order* and other prime-time shows.

WCUW was managed by a cigar-smoking lesbian who wouldn't allow Sinatra recordings to be played over her airwaves because of his mafia ties. JW was on staff and said some good things about me, resulting in my doing a jazz program there. My lieutenant colonel boss, when I asked if it would be all right, said, "Do the best jazz program you could." Dressed in uniform and giving PSAs about the Air Guard didn't sit well with her, especially when the local paper did an in-uniform feature article about me resulting in my being locked out of the building one Thursday when I was about to do my air shift.

We're In Constant Need (WICN) was where I volunteered for seven years at various times during the day, including a 3:00 to 6:00 a.m. program called *The Monday Morning Hog Report* that was listened to by night people, hookers, pimps, cops, firemen, and the like. JW and I would play jazz and shoot the shit about anything that was going on in the news and music.

On another program that was aired on Tuesday evening from 9:00 to 11:00 p.m., we interviewed jazz people like Ron Della Chiesa from WGBH, jazz vocalist Carol Sloane, Sonny Costanzo, Boston radio legend Norm Nathan, and the commander of the Air Guard Band. The local press honored us with a two-page feature with photos.

"Affirmative action" were buzzwords, and the state wanted us to bring in more minorities. And that resulted in my writing the storyboard and TV script for a locally produced minority-focused public service announcement. And the campaign worked to where I was able to fill up a newly acquired critical area with Hispanics from the project. All they needed to hear was the job required a top-secret clearance, and if they could get one, civilian government agencies who were also affirmative action conscious could hire them. Trying to find the name of the fathers of these kids is another story. A personnel specialist assigned to headquarters was Hispanic and knew what I was up against and somehow came to my rescue. And if that wasn't enough, none of the kids had a police record. Out of the ten, five got government jobs after teletype technical school.

There came the day before going to New York City to see the *City of Angels*. With my mother in tow, I was looking for a restaurant and, by the grace of God, found Gabby's car at a place we went to a couple of times, and then it happened.

There's Gabby sitting with the same friends I'd be with, only this time, it's not me. It's someone new, and she's laughing, having a good time. When I bought her table a round of drinks, she charged over to me and told me that was uncalled for. To this day, I don't know why I didn't tell her to fuck herself and simply take my mom to New York for the day. Knowing it's the end, I, with an intense ambivalence, agreed to meet her at the railroad station for our New York adventure.

Gotham

Under wraps of cold weather outerwear, our diddling sexual antics in orchestra seats stopped the show. It was an intense fitting end to our exhilarating nine months. The train ride back to New Haven was in silence, especially when she informed me she was engaged to the guy she was with the night before, and she wasn't even divorced yet.

The psychological cathexis (expulsion of psychic energy) of id, ego, and superego being spent was maddening. And with black bile and zero production while trying to make their precious four bodies a month, a major general was on the back of a one-star drunk, and he was on my boss's back, resulting in my signing unsatisfactory performance reports.

Clint, my fishing buddy, of Clint and Sandra fame, told me that Iva would take me back. Needing to get back to sanity and making up to do, I came home sobbing with my tail and tale 'tween my legs. That was the closest she and I have ever been, completely open to conversation about her. In the meantime, with the helplessness and hopelessness of getting better and knowing, just knowing I wasn't in God's favor, I clearly displayed a mind with serious issues. Off the cuff, I was told to check into Brighton Marine, where I would be seen by civilians at no cost. That's what I needed. Civilians and free!

Distressed, looking like shit in a disheveled uniform, shirt buttons open, tie thrown over my shoulder, I went to a dry cleaner and picked up a plastic bag. Bawling to where I was placed in an examining room away from the patients waiting, I tearfully told a young rebel MD I was gonna kill myself. When he asked about a plan, I told him of my auto-erotic ending with the plastic laundry bag. With a phone call, I was immediately put on medical leave. After which, he scheduled me to meet in four days with an AF psychiatrist seventy miles down the road and wrote a script for lithium. Other than "Tuebe's lost his mind," I couldn't imagine what was said about me at the base.

A grinding halt—no more oh dark-thirty trips to MEPS, no more high school food fights during my visits, no more under the gun, no more interaction with wonderful people. I was medicated and not having to work! You'd think relief.

Getting acclimated to the rigors of nothing and waiting for my trip to see the doc down the road, I was overcome by imagining the worse: not retirement-worthy and no steady income. With the rebel doc's medical record on me and my scraggly four-day growth of beard, the AF doctor compassionately recommended I be sent to Andrews Air Force Base for care, observation, evaluation, and retirement—a stay that I imagined would be a couple of days tops.

Weeks went by before I was sent to Malcolm Grow Medical Center, and from not eating, I was losing weight, enough to fit into a five-year-old blue-and-white seersucker suit.

Snazzy, when I finally did check into the hospital, I appeared quite stable to the shrink on duty, who put me on a level requiring little observation, allowing me endless privileges like going to the BX whenever I wanted.

With some serious issues, a female patient made a stink about my status and told the shrink off. The end of my coming and going had arrived, and I was in a locked unit with, among others, a major stationed at the Pentagon who swore he heard a drug buy going down in the commissary. Diagnosis? Schizophrenia! The AF wouldn't allow such behavior in the commissary in 1992. He must've been nuts.

During my stay, the ward ordered a bus to take some of us into the district. When I asked my Egyptian captain shrink if I could get my left ear pierced, he said, "No, you can't!" Seven of us mental patients roamed the district and took a tour I insisted upon at the VOA. As we were waiting for the tour to begin, a smoking, gaunt Willis Conover walked by.

Walking around the Aerospace Museum exhibits, our day in the big city ended. As we were waiting for the bus back to the base, I went to a kiosk and pierced my left ear with a tenor sax player playing. The next day, when the doc saw me and noticed my dangling accoutrement, he calmly said, "You pierced your ear," and walked over to his next patient.

While being titrated, I experienced a lot of maddening, unsettling seven-to-eight-minute cells of cycled bawling on a nurse's shoulder, after which I'd cycle into a mild manic state asking about getting into an operating theater to check out a procedure. It was here where a podiatrist who was to examine my feet and brief me on diabetic foot care wouldn't see me. I suspect it because I was on the ward. I waited for over three hours before going back to the ward.

Mentally, I madly ruminated and became obsessed with numbers, days 'til I went home for a couple of weeks, time, seconds, hours, minutes. It was sheer hell imagining I was lost in the system and I'd be there forever. You don't wanna have that obsession. An antipsychotic would've been quite appropriate, and things were getting grim.

When I finally went home for two weeks, I experienced no relief, just constant rumination over the hours and minutes till I went back to the hospital. No let up! Screaming numbers! One morning, I ran to my congressman's office and spoke to the office manager about the concern of my being at the hospital forever "'cuz they lost my records!" She called state headquarters. A well-respected high-ranking female NCO called the nerve center where all medical records are acted upon and was told to tell me, "Your record is coming up for review." It didn't ease my mind.

With my forehead pressed against the window of a forty-five-minute flight (on good old US Air from Providence, Rhode Island, to DC) and because I could no longer deal with this obsessing madness, I prayed a tearfully mournful, fretfully purging, fervent prayer that quite suddenly miraculously resulted in my feeling more stoned than ever; and with a renewed gait in my step, a glow of His presence and a God-loving exuberance, I danced out of that plane and even kissed the hand of a stewardess.

The next morning, my shrink says to me, "You're going home for good in two weeks!"

That was twenty-one years ago. You don't wanna know the rest of the story.

About the Author

"I was an easy birth. My father who was in the delivery room died of embarrassment."

Born in Bilgewater Falls, on the day of infamy, Tuebe'd Tzidid said to his cousin, "…Dan, I'm gonna see the world with my clarinet!" And he did. As a civilian he had a career in: broadcasting, producing and hosting jazz programs and coproducing award winning interviews with tunesmiths: Sammy Cahn, Arthur Hamilton, and David Mann.

There were over 50,000 young lives lost in Nam. His years in the AF and the medals he's been given have nothing to do with heroism. Tuebe'd says, "the real heroes are those victims who are still fighting the war in their head while consumed with awful memories. The rumination of which is devastating, paralyzing and hopefully is minimized with whatever Parke-Lily and the rest have come up with. Many of these heroes are unsung," Tuebe'd says, "living in boxes under big city underpasses, alleys, parking garages, dumpsters. And then there are those who are successfully retired, flirting with self-actualization and lest we forget the supportive noncombatants: Administrative, cooks, musicians, medical, etc.

"This is a memoir of my years in the AF from 1965-1992 (with a break in service). They're my stories and I'm sticking to 'em."